Going Small - A Guide to Lightweight Motorcycle Touring

"Take chances, make mistakes. That's how you grow. Pain nourishes your courage. You have to fail in order to practice being brave." - Mary Tyler Moore

Chapter One: The Stuff

"If you're never scared or embarrassed or hurt, it means you never take any chances."
- Julia Sorel

What is a lightweight motorcycle?

If you are looking at taking a long motorcycle trip, people will be more than happy to offer opinions on which bike you should take. Ultimately the choice is going to be up to you, the rider/traveler. This book is intended for small, lightweight bikes. Everything said here will also work for heavier motorcycles, reverse of which is not always true.

With that out of the way, what do I mean by "small, lightweight bikes?" I read a book written for lightweight motorcycle touring and the author commented he was riding a 650cc motorcycle weighing 400lbs, with gas but no luggage. In the USA, this is a small motorcycle though most of the rest of the world wouldn't think so. Personally I think of it as mid-sized. When I say small motorcycle I am thinking of engine sizes under 400ccs, with weights under 300lb. Even these motorcycles are the upper end of the bikes I think of as "light" since there are many people riding around the world right now (even two-up) on 250cc and 125cc motorcycles. You don't need to go big to go far.

Gear

"Do not spoil what you have by desiring what you have not; but remember what you have now was once among the things you only hoped for." - Epicurus

Camping

Shelter, along with food and water, is something every overland motorcycle traveler needs to think about. It is easy, if you have the budget, to find hotels or hostels all over the world to stay in, many with secure parking for the bike. If you are on a smaller budget, websites like Couchsurfing.com list people who either travel, or enjoy talking to travelers, and are willing to allow people to stay at their houses for a few nights. Details of how it works are listed on the website, so I won't go into it here, but it is a fantastic resource.

Of course, the romantic thing to do is find some quiet place, set up a tent and watch the stars drift overhead. For this you are going to have to pack a few extra things.

Camping near the Cumberland Falls, in Kentucky. Only place to see a Moonbow in the Western Hemisphere.

Tent

Space and weight are always the issue when traveling on a small motorcycle, and if you are committed to packing camping equipment then space and weight need to be considered carefully. Backpackers have all the cool technology, but it can be pricey. A cheaper option is a discount department store tent, or simply a tarp you can string up between trees. The tarp won't pack particularly small, but it can be used to wrap other, non-waterproof items and keep them dry on the motorcycle.

Remember when shopping for a tent the "person" rating often doesn't take into account anything other than the sleeping bag. No luggage or other stuff brought in to keep it safer or drier. If I want to bring everything inside I add a person to the space needed (so I travel with a two person tent when alone). When possible try to see how large the tent really is before purchase, or ask on motorcycle forums about tents others are using, and be prepared for a lot of conflicting information (it is the Internet, after all).

In the end you are going to have to pick a tent, based probably on some favorable reviews and cost, and give it a try. Most modern tents will serve for your journey unless you get one really too big or really too small. Hopefully this will be discovered on a test camp before the Big One.

Sleeping Bag

Sleeping bags, like tents, should be kept as small and light as possible. When considering a sleeping bag you need to think about when and where you are going to be using it. Sleeping bags are given temperature ratings, and the ones that are good for colder temperatures generally are heavier and pack larger than the ones for higher temperatures. So if you don't need a bag rated for -15f below, you shouldn't buy one. I used a 15f bag, with the occasional silk liner. I was never cold from one end of the Americas to the other.

Another important thing to consider about sleeping bags is the stuffing. Down bags generally pack the smallest, and are the warmest, but they don't tolerate getting wet very well and care must be taken to keep them dry. My down bag (Big Agnes Lost Ranger) is slightly waterproof, so it can take a little water, but others are much more sensitive. Synthetic bags are more immune to water (as in, getting wet doesn't ruin them but they still take days to dry), but are much heavier and bulkier. Most camping stores/outfitters have sales people experienced with the various types of bags, and talking to them can help you choose the correct one.

Mattress

Many riders skip a sleeping pad as unneeded luxury. Piled leaves, or a slight depression dug into the ground is all they want. Others use hammock tents to avoid the need (adding the need for trees). I prefer to pack a pad for the extra comfort at the end of the riding day and use one with a down filling to provide extra warmth in colder climates. You lose more heat into the ground, if you are sleeping without a pad, than you risk losing from an inadequate sleeping bag.

If you are shopping for a pad, backpacking stores are again the place to look for small, light models. If you are looking to spend a little (or a lot) less than you can obtain a firm (called a closed foam) pad in a discount department store. These are going to be larger and heavier than the expensive versions, but the cost savings could be worth it (my pad, which I have to blow up myself, packs to about the size of a soda can and cost $20 more than the roll of foam at the local discount chain).

If you don't like the big foam roll, you can use an air mattress (which I did for several years and still do on occasion) that requires an air pump to inflate. This means you also have to pack an air pump, but even the pair of items may be smaller than the roll of foam. Your bike might be able to run the air pump from a 12 volt plug, or you can purchase a battery operated version (make sure you are carrying extra batteries).

Camping in Alaska with a hammock tent. Very comfortable, and you don't need a mattress, though you will need a couple trees.

Cooking

There are several different options for eating on the road. Many solo travelers prefer to find local places to eat, to let them meet and interact with other people. Some people carefully plan and pack dehydrated meals for easy preparation, others stop in grocery stores to buy either ready to eat food or food that they can prepare and cook later. Like so many parts of long motorcycle trips this is something each rider or group of riders will have to work out for themselves, and it's important to try a few different things to find what works best before leaving home for The Big One. I found it best to pack several snacks I could eat cold, such as sausage or granola, and actually cook when I camped in the evenings. If I stayed in a town or hotel I would find somewhere local to eat. When in places I couldn't find food I could prepare myself (I am by no means a chef), I would eat out more.

If you are serious about cooking on the road there are several excellent books on one-pan cooking. Taking the books along might not work well (they don't pack well), but favorite recipes copied down are a different story.

Cook With

If you are going to cook food you will need some sort of heat. The purist, simplest thing to use is fire. You can find wood, or at least something to burn, most places in the world where people live, though it is trickier in some places and you might have to burn non-traditional items (dried cow and sheep feces are popular in some areas).

I prefer to cook over fire. I carry skewers for hot dogs or bratwurst, and they double as a grill when I need one. I also pack a small Coleman gas burning stove since I like a warm drink on chilly mornings and am too lazy when I wake up to get the fire going again. The stove also allows me to quickly make something warm for lunch on the side of the road. I still enjoy sitting by the fire at night as the sun sets, and using the stove when I have a fire just seems silly.

Cook In

Whether you are cooking over a fancy, high-tech burner or a fire as your barbarian ancestors did, you need something to hold the food. You can make a rotating spit with smaller sticks (clean off the bark), or pack a single pot and balance it on rocks next to the fire.

If you are willing to pack more in the way of pots and pans, various brands of nesting sets are available. These fit inside each other, so they take up less room in the luggage (or backpack, again they were designed for backpackers). With more variety in the utensils you can prepare a greater variety of dishes, which can be a bonus if you are on the road long enough.

I like to travel with a small pot which came with a vented lid. The lid allows me to pour water out when I make noodles, without dumping the noodles all over. For longer trips I also pack a small frying pan, which I can use for pancakes, sausage or bacon. I also bring along a roll of aluminum foil (good for reheating, or making hobo meals), and a set of skewers (for hot dogs or brats, and also good for building a grilling or cooking surface over a fire).

Food

When traveling, how much of what food to carry is a very personal choice. I tend to carry lots of snacks and ingredients for two or three meals. When shopping I think about the weather outside, both for what I might want to eat and for how long it will last.

Small motorcycles won't have refrigerators, so things like cold cuts or meat for cooking need to be used up right away. If you are riding in colder weather, they will last longer, but buying several pounds of anything is usually a bad idea (unless you have a big group). Granola bars, chips, fruit (be careful when packing since they bruise), jerky or sausage (some sausage doesn't require refrigeration, read the label) all will keep on a motorcycle. For sandwiches I found soft tortillas work better than bread, since it can't be crushed in the food bag, but occasionally buying rolls for immediate use can turn into a treat.

For warm food, the easiest thing to make is soup or something that comes in a metal can. Place the whole can into hot water to heat it up and you won't have to wash the pot after. Remember to remove the label first, and stir frequently. Instant noodles (such as Ramen) can be prepared quickly and easily, and made better if you take the time to add fresh veggies or pre-cooked meat.

Clothing

Whether you are camping out or staying in hotels, finding restaurants or cooking over a fire, you will need to pack clothes. Once you get over the need to wear clean underwear everyday (or get good at daily laundry) you might be surprised at how little clothing you actually need to pack.

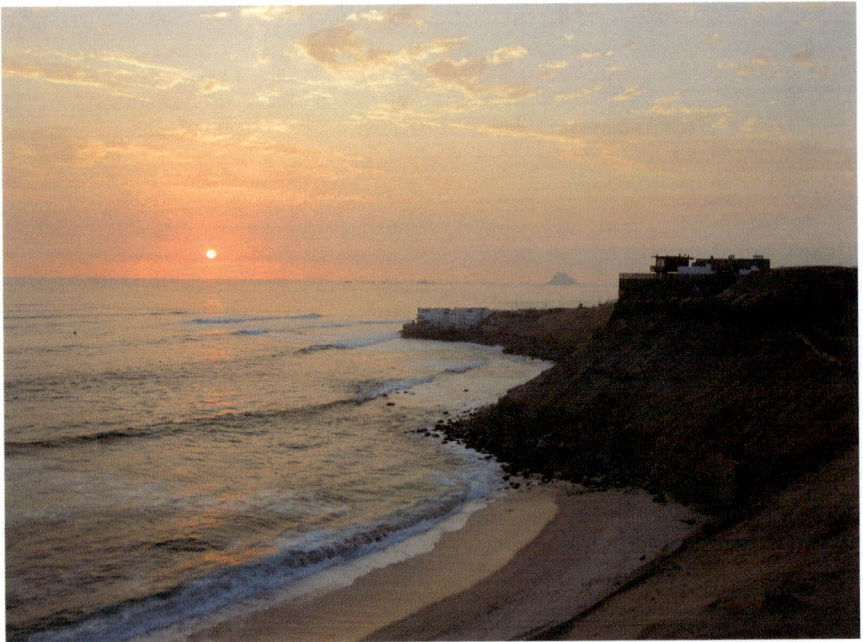

A beach south of Lima, Peru

On the Bike

On the bike I always wear armored motorcycle pants and jacket, a full face helmet (actually a modular one, so it's easy to flip up and smile at people), boots that cover my ankles, and gloves. Some riders prefer leather pants and jackets (the pants also providing off the motorcycle wear), but I prefer modern textiles. Textiles are usually better vented for hot weather, and waterproof so I don't need to carry extra rain gear or deal with clothing changes when the rain closes in.

Mesh jackets and pants are available, in both leather and textile, and they are considerably cooler than their non-mesh counterparts (the textile jackets and pants more so), which can be a boon in the hot dry places of the world, but a serious problem when it gets colder. If you are planning to only bring mesh, also plan on layers.

For prolonged cold (or even cool, say under 60f) I have heated liners. I know 60f doesn't seem that cold, but the goal is to avoid feeling chilled at all. Occasional cool feels fine, and even refreshing, but if it goes on too long and you start to feel cold, you start to lose body heat, which is a bad thing. Stop somewhere you can warm up again (preferably with your coat off, the layers will hold in the cold just like they hold in the heat).

Off the Bike

The only two things I carry for off the bike wear are a pair of pants (so I can not wear the armored motorcycle pants) and lightweight shoes (which double as shower wear). I will pack a pair of shorts for swimming or sleep wear, if I think they will get used.

The most I will carry is three changes of clothes: Three t-shirts, three pairs of socks and three underwear. Synthetic is better, since it is usually wicking and dries quickly when it gets wet. I have also been known to carry more pairs of socks, since dry ones are always nice to put on.

For colder weather I have long underwear (synthetic and wicking again) and a long sleeve shirt. With the jacket and liner, this set of clothes has managed to keep me warm in the snow and only a little melted in the desert. It all fit into a small compression bag, except the shoes.

The Bike

"In the end, we decide if we're remembered for what happened to us or for what we did with it." - Randy K. Milholland

Size

This book is about small, light motorcycles. Motorcycles with engine sizes under 400cc. But really,the smaller the bike the bigger the story. To ride anywhere (and everywhere) in the world, you don't really need anything over 250cc.

Many riders planning long overland trips (going to Baja, for example) prefer to use dual sport or off road bikes. They have longer suspension travel and it is easier to get special off road tires. They are also geared lower, which means they are easier to get unstuck, but have lower top speeds. Yamaha's XT225, a very popular small overland motorcycle, won't go 60mph without modification but would laugh at sand that slows my street bike to a crawl. I choose a street bike because it easily manages freeway speeds even with luggage. It wasn't as good off road as a true dual sport or off road bike would have been, but the bike was so light it is ride-able despite its limitations.

When choosing your motorcycle you need to consider where you want to go on it.

New or Old

When you roll up to a gas station on a small bike, loaded with a tent, a few other possessions and a license plate from far away, you are already going to be attracting attention. When you mention the bike is older than you are (or at least was built before you were legally able to ride it), eyebrows will raise further.

Older motorcycles will need more regular maintenance, and probably more work before leaving, than a new one. There may also be difficulty in locating the correct parts. In smaller countries the locals use whatever is available, but here in the USA mechanics will go to great lengths to find original parts (passing the costs on to you). On the other side of the equation, if you have problems in a small town in Ecuador you have a much better chance of the local mechanic being able to get you back on the road again.

Of course, on a newer bike your odds of being broken down in a small town in Ecuador drop considerably, so it is a matter of personal comfort. Either way you will want to bring along tools appropriate both for your bike and your ability to work on it, and the service manual. You might not be able use the manual, but the mechanic who is helping you might.

For a minimum of tools, you should be able to perform regular maintenance (oil changes, valve adjustments if the trip is long enough that you will need one, and tire changes or patching) and some small spares, such as fuses, light bulbs and spark plugs.

Luggage

I know people who have invested thousands on dollars in their motorcycle luggage. Special boxes, special racks, loops for straps on the inside and out. Waterproof liners, since the $600 box isn't already waterproof, and another one for the other side.

I also know people who have bought two identical backpacks from a discount bin, sewn them together and thrown them over the back of the bike.

I started with those backpacks, and they served me well for a couple years of nearly constant travel. I finally got rid of them when, after a heavy rainstorm, they stretched and hit the exhaust pipe. Now, with a little more money to invest, I have a set of throw over soft bags from a company called Ortlieb. They are waterproof, have plenty of room (the larger the bag, the more you will carry. Keep the bags small), and have held up to some serious abuse. They also cost considerably less than aluminum hard boxes but you will have to find somewhere else to put stickers.

Soft bags are lighter, hard bags provide more protection for their contents and for the bike if it falls over. Waterproofness is something they both may or may not have (and it doesn't have much to do with the cost). I used soft bags because I already owned them and they were much lighter than the hard bags I also owned.

I tried various types of hard luggage, but in the end used soft bags. The weight savings was worth it.

Weight penalty

The weight penalty is the cost, in weight, of carrying something on your motorcycle. When traveling in a car, we rarely think about how heavy our camping gear is, and on a larger touring bike (while it is something you should be thinking carefully about) you usually only give it enough consideration to keep the bike balanced. On smaller bikes this needs more planning, since the available carrying capacity is less.

This isn't a bad thing. The larger the bags you have on the bike the more stuff you tend to carry but you can go on a long, enjoyable trip with much less equipment and not even notice what you didn't bring. It does take some practice and planning, but in the long run makes for a much more enjoyable journey.

The available carrying capacity of your motorcycle is the Gross Vehicle Weight Rating (Listed as the GVWR in the owner's manual) minus the Wet Weight. Most motorcycles list, both online and in the owners manual, something called the Dry Weight, which is the weight of the motorcycle without oil, gas or other fluids. On a larger bike you can add about 50lbs to the dry weight to get an idea of the actual weight. Smaller motorcycles carry less gas and oil, so you can add less, about 6 pounds per gallon of gas and .75 pounds per quart or liter of oil (oil weight varies a lot, so that is approximate). My 250cc street bike carried about 17 pounds of fluids.

Once you know the carrying capacity of your bike, you need to subtract the weight of you in your riding gear. This is going to be a lot heavier than you on the scale in the morning, so suit up and get the correct weight. I gain a bit over 30 pounds with jacket, liners, boots and helmet. It sure doesn't feel like that much.

Now you know the remaining carrying capacity of your motorcycle. It will look pretty small, but don't worry. It will be enough.

When you are looking at adding things to your luggage (and don't forget to weigh the luggage itself, those soft bags start looking better and better), think about the weight you are adding to the bike as a percentage. If you have 10% in clothes, 30% in camping, 30% in tools and spares (they are always heavy) and 20% in cooking equipment and food, you are still underweight. It won't be that easy, but thinking about it like this allows you to consider everything you are carrying as a complete item, rather than "Is this 20 pound tent too heavy?"

The less you use of your weight limit, the better the bike will handle, the longer the tires, chain and sprockets will last, the less gas you will use. In the long run, less definitely works out to more.

Chapter Two: The Rider

"Maps encourage boldness. They're like
cryptic love letters. They make anything
seem possible." - Mark Jenkins

Three Rules of Going Small

"Even the fear of death is nothing compared to the fear of not having lived authentically and fully." - Frances Moore Lappe

Keep it Simple

Keep it Simple. Just about everyone has heard that phrase at some point in their life. With small motorcycles it applies to just about everything. Simple motorcycle, simple luggage (no need for $2500 worth of titanium side bags and rack), simple roads (six lane interstate? Pass). Like life, motorcycling is easy to over think. You have to be aware of the danger, it will sneak up on you.

If you don't use it, Don't Pack It

This may be related to the first rule, but most things are. I met a rider who was carrying a wood-burning stove with him. He had been on the road for two weeks and hadn't used it. He also had a gas burning stove, which he had used "a couple times," but he really loved that wood-burning one. Got it out and showed me, explaining he had tried it at home and it worked great. I pointed out that, if he was going to burn wood, he could just make a fire, but he insisted the stove was better.

Even though he hadn't been using it.

It is easy to get caught up in new gadgets, new toys, and if you spend any time in outfitting stores or going to expos you can find yourself overloaded with amazing gizmos. Some of these are truly useful items, but most aren't. Try a couple of short trips with your gear before the Big One and find out what you really use. If you don't use it, don't pack it no matter how cool or useful it might be. This includes tools, bring what you need for regular maintenance of the motorcycle. If you need major repairs you will probably find all the help you need on the road.

Getting my flat tire fixed in the mountains. Cost about a dollar.

Pace is Everything

On a small bike, even one capable of 80 or 100mph, it is usually better to stay off the main roads and explore the smaller, quieter state and local roads. I find the people are more friendly, the food better and the camping cheaper the further I get from a divided highway, and the lower speeds mean better gas mileage (since saving money equals more time on the road), less wear and tear on the motorcycle and more chances to enjoy the journey. While in the Yukon I met someone from Israel who had flown to Alaska, purchased a motorcycle and was riding south. He planned to be in San Diego in five days, a distance I took more than a month to cover. He might have made it, but he sure didn't see anything along the way.

Stop frequently. Sit in a park for a soda and snack, or next to a river on the side of the road. Slow Down.

Money

Traveling, like most things in life, costs money. And overland travel tends to cost a little more than a weekend road trip. Some people manage to earn money while on the road, but most travelers save up a certain amount and then hit the road.

Since the funds are limited, anything that can reduce the costs results in more travel time. In this, more than anything else, small motorcycles excel. Tires are less expensive, they get better fuel economy, and they can be cheaper to ship (mainly by air, but this is getting less so as air companies install "minimum weights" on motorcycles) when you run out of continent.

Also, if you are on a small bike instead of the latest large dual-sport adventure bike with all the boxes and lights, you attract less attention in countries where there are checkpoints or police who may need...fees...to allow you to continue. When I was traveling through Mexico and Central America I passed without problems through areas where other riders (and even a couple in a truck) were stopped and fined for one thing or other. One the other hand you attract more of the good attention from the locals, since you are riding a motorcycle much like their own.

Lastly, if it all goes horribly wrong and you find yourself on the side of the road with a hole in your engine, or a cracked frame from too rough of a road, walking away from the small, inexpensive motorcycle doesn't cause the financial damage as if you were in the same position with a $17,000 adventure bike.

The road out of Abancay, Peru

Why Light?

Lightweight motorcycles are all about size of the bike. This book recommends engine sizes under 400cc (with around 250 as ideal), and a weight (with oil and gas, but no luggage) of under 300lbs. With this, even with a street (non-dirt) bike you should be able to go anywhere a big bike can go and manage it at a fraction of the cost.

Consider just this. A 2012 BMW R1200GSA, probably the dream bike of many adventure motorcyclists, claims 51mpg on the website (Most actual riders I've asked report upper 30s to mid 40s on previous years R1200GSA's). My 1981 250 actually got 80mpg unloaded, mid 60s with all my luggage on it, and still weighed less (for when it fell over and I had to pick it up) than an unloaded big bike. And it would manage United States interstate speeds, if for some reason you wanted or needed to ride very far on the interstate. A full set of tires before I left was $150 installed, and insurance for a year was under $100. The bike cost $65 (I had to install a new battery and clean the carburetor). That is a lot of money for traveling I just saved.

Now, if you don't want to buy an older bike, a new, small engine motorcycle will still cost less than $5,000 (if you look at recent used motorcycles, rather than 30 year old ones, you can cut that in half), which still leaves a lot of extra money for gas, food and lodging somewhere far away from home.

Why Go?

People often say "The world is getting smaller every day." What they really mean isn't that the world is getting smaller. That's impossible. They mean it is easier to travel from place to place, easier to communicate with people who are far away, and they are wrong.

Not just in the physical sense, although that is obvious. The world isn't getting smaller. People fly from place to place, take shuttles or taxis to hotels, stay in all-inclusive resorts. Have Skype Meetings. They don't really experience the world, and barely experience parts of it.

Overland travel, especially on a motorcycle, forces you to experience every mile that connects one place to another in a real, visceral sense. The heat, the cold, the wind and rain, the sun, the smells, the waves of people on the sides of the road or in the fields, the smiles when you stop and they come over to look at you and the bike (even the little bikes, so like the bikes they might own). Even with no more than a few words in common, the sense of community, of sharing the world with those people is worth a hundred all-inclusive vacation destinations.

It is always easy to find a reason not to go, to delay going. The bike isn't ready. I need to read a new guidebook I just found. Work is really crazy right now. There really is only one reason to go - the whole world is out there.

Appendix A

The Packing List

This is the list of equipment I brought with me when I rode the Americas, with notes about what I lost, what I kept, and what I replaced things with.

Camping

Ozark Trail 3 person tent **(replaced)** Was seven years old when I left, and started leaking just before I entered Canada. I made a mistake and replaced it with an impulse purchase.

Nomad Tenere Two Person Tent **(replaced)** Truly an impressive tent, I could walk around in it, but much too large for my bike and this trip.

Hennessey Expedition Hammock Small, comfortable, and (once I got the hang of it) easy to put up and take down, my only complaint was, without trees, it just wasn't that comfortable.

Synthetic Sleeping Bag **(replaced)** I don't know the brand, but it was nearly as old as I was. I was just unwilling to upgrade, but in the end it wasn't up to the cold and I had to get a new one.

Big Agnes Lost Ranger 15f A down bag with a compartment on the bottom to hold the sleeping pad, it was a huge improvement. I was never cold again.

Ozark Trail Air Mattress **(replaced)** There wasn't anything wrong with my air mattress, and it was amazingly comfortable, but when I got the new sleeping bag I got the matching pad.

Big Agnes Primafill Sleeping Pad
This I had to blow up manually, which at
altitude wasn't much fun. But it was
comfortable and warm.

Cooking

Coleman Sportsman **(replaced)** Small,
with no assembly needed, all I can tell you
about this is I couldn't find a replacement
when it failed to appear after I shipped it
further ahead on my route.

MSR Simmerlite Stove I got the
Simmerlite because it claimed to be able to
control the heat, rather than "all on" or
"all off." The claims were sort of true, but
I can't recommend it.

GSI One Person Cookset **(replaced)** A
simple pot and bowl arrangement, with room
inside for utensils. Hard to find anything
better, and this was also lost with my
Coleman cooker.

Ozark Trail Cookset A cheap
replacement, it did well on the trip, but
wasn't as easy to pack.

Tools

Tire Irons Make sure you know how
they work.

Compressor Didn't really need it,
except for the side of the road repairs.
Worth it for that.

Stock Tool Set My bike, being older,
came with enough tools to take the whole
thing apart. Very helpful.

Large Vice Grips For stuck things,
banging things, and looking mean.

Ratchet Set Not really needed, but
handy. If you don't have one make sure you

have enough of the correct wrenches to loosen nut/bolt combinations (the large vice might do in a pinch).

Impact Screwdrivers Which doubled as regular screwdrivers.

Small Hammer/Hatchet Combination Also good for tent stakes and firewood.

Multi-Tool This was in my backpack, and I used it constantly. Buy a good one, it will be worth it. I have a Wave.

Spares

Spare Tubes One for each tire, and patches to repair the tubes. (Obviously, if you have tubeless tires, you just need the repair kit).

Spark Plugs I carried one, but a full set of replacements would be recommended.

Cables Everything on my bike is controlled by a cable (except the rear brake, which has a rod). I had replacement cables for all functions run through the frame, so if a cable broke (which two did, front brake and clutch) the replacement on the roadside would be simple.

Clothing

Shoei Multitec Helmet Modular, so I could show my face without taking it off, it was a little heavy. And black, which made it hotter. But it fit my head well and held up.

First Gear Kilimanjaro Jacket Waterproof and well vented, it also has a about a hundred pockets. Most of them were empty, so I could lock it to the bike.

First Gear HT Air Mesh Pants I chose mesh pants to help with the heat, and it was a good choice. I didn't use a mesh jacket to avoid getting too cold, but in the end I think it would have been fine, and a lot cooler.

Warm'n'Safe Heated Jacket Liner For when it got really cold, was very handy. I had a regulator, instead of just an on/off switch, which I prefer but probably isn't needed.

Ecco Hiking Boots A boot I used for work, they covered my ankles for support and were very comfortable for walking.

Three pairs of Gloves Various makes, one for hot weather, one for cold (which were also heated), and medium set. All were waterproof (When I left home, anyway).

Vibram Five Toe Shoes For when it was too hot for the boots, and for use in showers.

Underarmor Cold Gear, Top and Bottoms For cold weather wear.

Merino Wool Sweater Shipped home, I never wore it.

Five Pair Smartwool Socks Three standard pair, and two short pair with five toes.

Thick Wool Socks Shipped home, since I wasn't wearing them either.

Seal Skin Oversocks initially bought because my boots leaked a little, they became my cold weather socks.

Two Bandanas Generally useful for cold weather neck protection, dust filtering, or wiping off your face.

Three Short Sleeve T-Shirts For general wear. It became four when I bought another I liked.

One Long Sleeve T-Shirt Also for general wear, when it was a little colder.

One pair of Khaki Pants For wear off

the bike, to give myself a break from the motorcycle pants.

Electronics

Canon Elph 780IS Not a fancy camera, but 12.2mp and capable of HD video. I also had a spare battery.

Kindle The model names have changed since I bought it, but it is now the 3G Keyboard. Amazon's Whispernet Internet service is available in most countries, so I could get email and Facebook on the Kindle, and the battery lasts for weeks.

Nexus S Phone The Nexus, which was the latest Google phone when I left, came unlocked so I could put SIM cards in from other countries. In the end I didn't, but it was still nice to know I could.

HP Pavilion Tablet PC **(replaced)** My primary laptop for the year before I left, I shipped it home after becoming worried about all the sandy beaches I was sitting on, or something else happening to it.

HP Netbook Mini-110 Bought on the road I didn't research it much past the price, but it was smaller, lighter and had six times the battery life, so I was very happy.

WD 500GB External Hard Drive For backing up pictures, and stored somewhere else on the bike. Whenever I could I also backed up everything online, using smugmug.com.

Other

Folding Chair Since it's nice to have somewhere to sit.

Blue the Bear A plush doll, good for making friends in far away places.

Made in the USA
Lexington, KY
13 February 2013